Who lives here?

A Random House PICTUREBACK®

Animals live almost everywhere.
They hide in the grass or under rocks.
They nest in treetops or in burrows underground.
Many animals build homes. Others live in homes
another animal once built. And some animals
don't have homes at all. They roam about in the open,
searching for food. You may live near a garden
or meadow, or visit a pond, or go to the mountains.
If you do, watch closely, listen quietly,
and find out who lives there.

Who lives here?

Animals of the Pond, Forest, Prairie, Desert, Mountains, Meadow, and Swamp

by Dot and Sy Barlowe

Random House New York

Copyright © 1978 by Random House, Inc. All rights reserved under International and Pan-American Copyright Conventions.
Published in the United States by Random House, Inc., New York, and simultaneously in Canada by Random House of Canada Limited, Toronto.
Library of Congress Cataloging in Publication Data: Barlowe, Dorothy. Who lives here? SUMMARY: Introduces the homes a wide variety of animals make for their families.
1. Animals, Habitations of—Juvenile literature. [1. Animals—Habitations] I. Barlowe, Sy, joint author. II Title. QL756.B35 1980 591.56'4 79-27494.
ISBN: 0-394-83667-7 (B.C.); 0-394-83740-1 (trade); 0-394-93740-6 (lib. bdg.)
Manufactured in the United States of America   A B C D E F G H I J   2 3 4 5 6 7 8 9 0

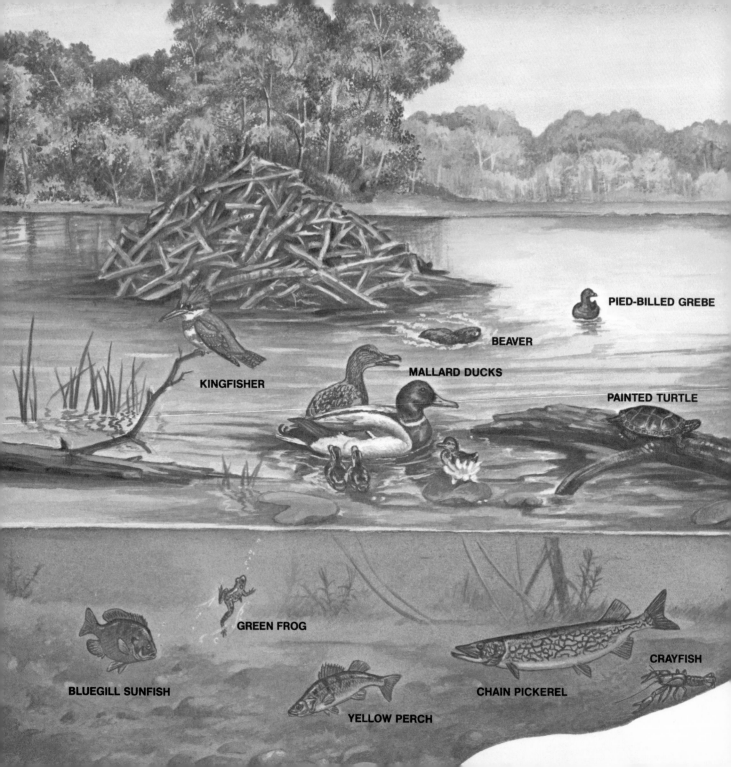

PIED-BILLED GREBE

BEAVER

KINGFISHER

MALLARD DUCKS

PAINTED TURTLE

GREEN FROG

BLUEGILL SUNFISH

YELLOW PERCH

CHAIN PICKEREL

CRAYFISH

RED-WINGED BLACKBIRD

MUSKRAT

BEAVER

DRAGONFLY

BULLFROG

A pond is a home for many animals. Some animals live in the water. Others build homes in the mud or tall grass at the edge of the pond. Though frogs can live on land, they spend much of their time in the water. Dragonflies fly above the pond, hunting insects for food. The muskrat builds a home of reeds and mud in shallow water. Mallard ducks hide their nests in the tall grass beside the pond.

Beavers use deep water to protect themselves from enemies. They make a "beaver pond" by cutting down logs and branches and building a dam across a stream.

Beavers' homes are called lodges. They are made from branches covered with mud, stones, and plants.

BEAVER DAM

Underwater tunnels lead into the lodge. The beavers can swim through them without being seen.

The lodge has a dry room above the level of the water. Underwater, beavers store soft wood and bark for their winter supply of food.

GREBE ON FLOATING NEST

The female grebe lays her eggs in a floating nest that she builds from plants. If she leaves the nest, she hides her eggs under more plants.

The painted turtle sleeps through the winter in the mud at the edge of the pond. It doesn't come out until spring.

PAINTED TURTLE IN WINTER

KINGFISHER DIVING

The belted kingfisher dives into the pond and catches fish in its beak.

Belted kingfishers do not build nests as other birds do. Instead, both the males and females use their feet and heavy beaks to dig a burrow in the bank of the pond. They raise their babies in a large space at the end of the tunnel.

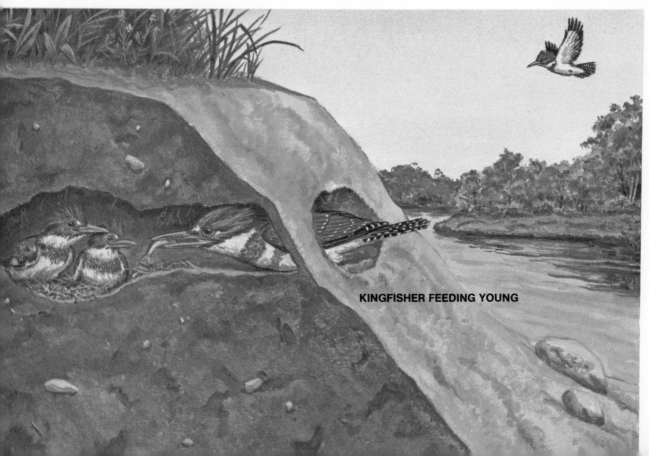

KINGFISHER FEEDING YOUNG

The forest provides homes for many animals. Squirrels and birds live in nests in the topmost branches of the trees. Salamanders and snails hide under rocks and tree stumps. The gray fox makes its den in a hollow tree, a cave, or an underground burrow. Some forest animals do not build homes. The white-tailed deer travels around, eating twigs, leaves, nuts, and grasses. It sleeps hidden among the shrubs or bushes.

OWL

MONARCH
BUTTERFLY

RACCOON

SQUIRREL'S NEST

GRAY SQUIRREL

BAT

FLYING SQUIRREL

BOBCAT

CHIPMUNK

After a tree dies, it slowly becomes hollow. But many more years often pass before it falls down. Until it falls, a hollow tree is the home of many creatures. Smaller ones live in hollow limbs. Larger animals—opossums, porcupines, and bobcats—live in the trunk. Tree homes are mostly ready-made. But some animals make their nests more comfortable by bringing in leaves and grass.

BISON

BADGER

SAGE GROUSE

PRAIRIE DOGS

PRAIRIE RATTLESNAKE

Prairies, or grasslands, stretch for miles and miles. Many different kinds of animals live there. The bison and the pronghorn antelope do not have permanent homes. They go wherever there is plenty of grass to eat. Other animals hide in the tall grass, and many live in burrows underground.

PRONGHORN ANTELOPE

MEADOWLARK

WHITE-TAILED JACK RABBIT

BOBCAT

BURROWING OWL

STRIPED SKUNKS

PACK RAT

Prairie dogs live in large "prairie dog towns." These are made up of many burrows. Each burrow has tunnels that lead to rooms for sleeping and storing food. When a prairie dog senses danger, it gives a loud bark to warn its neighbors. Then all the prairie dogs hurry underground.

PRAIRIE DOGS' BURROWS

COYOTE AND CUBS

Coyotes often raise their babies in dens that once belonged to another animal.

The burrowing owl can dig its own underground home. But often it lives in an empty prairie dog burrow.

This is not always good. Burrowing owls sometimes eat young prairie dogs. And prairie dogs will sometimes eat the burrowing owl's eggs.

BURROWING OWL IN PRAIRIE DOG BURROW

RED-TAILED HAWK

BLACK-TAILED
JACK RABBIT

COLLARED
PECCARY

RATTLESNAKE

COLLARED LIZARD

ROADRUNNER

The desert is very hot and dry. Some desert animals sleep during the day to protect themselves from the hot sun. They come out at night to hunt for food.

There is not much water in the desert. But desert animals get most of the water they need from eating plants and seeds.

ELF OWL

COYOTE

CACTUS WREN

SPOTTED SKUNK

GILA MONSTER

DESERT TORTOISE

PACK RAT

The kit fox digs its den in soft desert soil. It makes several openings so it can get in or out of the den quickly.

During daylight, the kangaroo rat fills the opening of its burrow with earth to keep the heat out.

The trap-door spider digs a burrow, too. It makes a trap door to hide the opening. The spider waits behind the door for an insect to come by. Then it opens the door, grabs the insect, and eats it inside the burrow.

KIT FOX

KANGAROO RAT

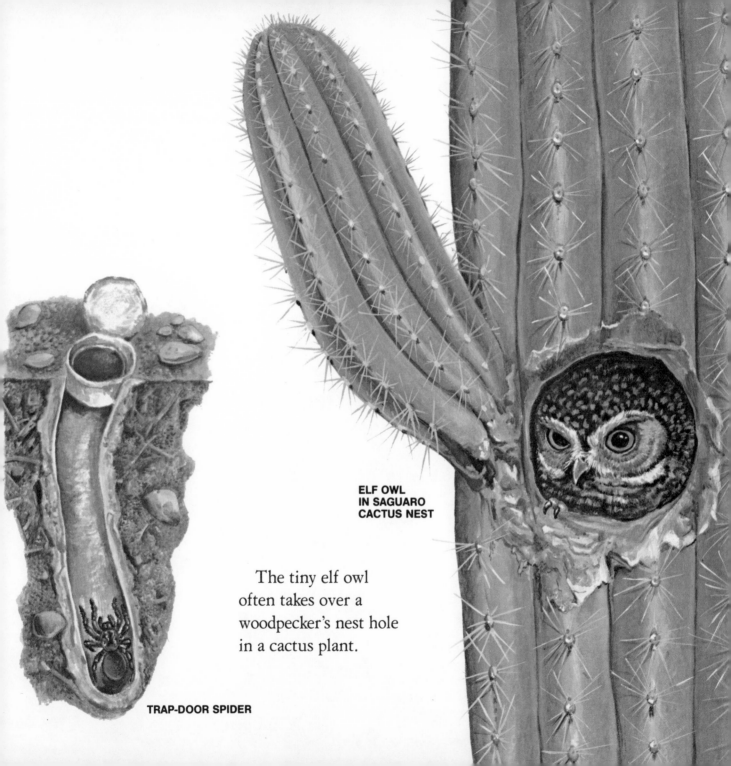

**ELF OWL
IN SAGUARO
CACTUS NEST**

The tiny elf owl
often takes over a
woodpecker's nest hole
in a cactus plant.

TRAP-DOOR SPIDER

Mountain goats and sheep roam about searching for food. They have no trouble climbing up and down the steep, rocky mountains. The little pika is as sure-footed as the goats and sheep. It makes its home in the spaces between rocks, where it stores grass and leaves for winter. The yellow-bellied marmot also lives among the rocks. It lines its nest with grass.

MOUNTAIN LION

PIKA

ELK

YELLOW-BELLIED
MARMOT

PIKA

GOLDEN EAGLE

MOUNTAIN GOATS

MOUNTAIN SHEEP

CLARK'S
NUTCRACKER

BLACK BEARS

MOUNTAIN LION AND CUBS

GOLDEN EAGLE AND EAGLETS

The golden eagle builds a huge nest
on rocky cliffs or in large trees.
This nest, called an aerie, is a big
platform made of sticks and grasses,
vines and plant stems. Eagles use
the same nests year after year.

Mountain lions usually live in caves. But sometimes they make their dens underneath a pile of loose rocks.

The black bear also lives in a cave, though it will sometimes scoop out a hole under a fallen tree. The black bear sleeps through the winter. The bear cubs are born in midwinter, before the mother bear is fully awake.

SNOWSHOE HARE

BLACK BEAR AND CUBS

MONARCH
BUTTERFLY

HORNETS'
NEST

HONEYBEE

ANT

SKUNKS

HOVER FLY

SPITTLE
BUG

FOX

GARDEN SPIDER

SNAIL

GRAY SQUIRREL

ROBIN

GARTER SNAKE

WHITE-FOOTED MOUSE

A meadow, or field, is an open place with short grasses, many wild flowers, and low shrubs.

A garden with a lawn is like a meadow. But it is planned and taken care of by people. Many of the same animals live either in gardens or in meadows.

Moles dig very fast through the earth, making tunnels as they search for food. Their eyesight is poor, but their noses tell them where to find food. Moles eat harmful insects and grubs. But gardeners don't like the ugly ridges and molehills that moles make when they tunnel through a garden.

Earthworms help gardeners. Their small tunnels allow air to get into the soil and keep it loose. Earthworms bring pieces of leaves into the soil, making it richer. Many birds and animals that live in fields and gardens eat earthworms.

MOLE

EARTHWORMS

Most ants live in big underground colonies. An ant colony has many tunnels and rooms. Some rooms are nurseries for raising babies. Others are used for storing food.

EGGS

FOOD

LARVAE

PUPAE IN COCOONS

ANHINGA

RED-HEADED
WOODPECKER

FOX SQUIRREL

RACCOON

PENINSULAR
TURTLE

MARSH RABBIT

A swamp or marsh is a warm, wet place where trees and plants grow in shallow water. The roseate spoonbill makes a nest of sticks in low trees or shrubs. Raccoons usually live in hollow logs, though they will sometimes live in caves near the swamp. Most of the animals that live in the swamp are good swimmers. The marsh rabbit is a very good swimmer. It builds a nest among the tall swamp grasses.

IBIS

SWALLOW-TAILED KITE

EGRET

ROSEATE
SPOONBILL

ALLIGATOR

COTTONMOUTH

PURPLE
GALLINULE

Alligators live both in the water and on land. An alligator builds its nest on land. The nest is made of plants. The eggs are hidden inside until they hatch.

ALLIGATOR AND NEST

Wherever animals live—in the swamp, the meadow, or the mountains—most need a place to raise their babies, to hide from their enemies, and to find their food.